London College of Music

CW00377215

Grade Two

Classical Guitar Playing

Compiled by
Tony Skinner, Raymond Burley and Amanda Cook
on behalf of

Registry of Guitar Tutors

Printed and bound in Great Britain

A CIP record for this publication is available from the British Library
ISBN: 978-1-905908-12-7

Published by Registry Publications

Registry Mews, Wilton Rd, Bexhill, Sussex, TN40 1HY

Cover artwork by Danielle Croft. Design by JAK Images.
Music engraving by Alan J Brown, Chaz Hart, Mark Houghton,
Dmitry Milovanov and Oskay Hoca.

Compiled for **LCM Exams** by

www.RGT.org

INTRODUCTION _____

This publication is part of a progressive series of ten handbooks, primarily intended for candidates considering taking the London College Of Music examinations in classical guitar playing. However, given each handbook's wide content of musical repertoire and associated educational material, the series provides a solid foundation of musical education for any classical guitar student – whether intending to take an examination or not. Whilst the handbooks can be used for independent study, they are ideally intended as a supplement to individual or group tuition.

Examination entry

An examination entry form is provided at the rear of each handbook. This is the only valid entry form for the London College Of Music classical guitar examinations.

Please note that *if the entry form is detached and lost, it will not be replaced under any circumstances* and the candidate will be required to obtain a replacement handbook to obtain another entry form.

Editorial information

Examination performances must be from this handbook edition. All performance pieces should be played in full, including all repeats shown; the pieces have been edited specifically for examination use, with all non-required repeat markings omitted.

Tempos, fingering and dynamic markings are for general guidance only and need not be rigidly adhered to, providing an effective musical result is achieved.

Pick-hand fingering is normally shown on the stem side of the notes:
p = thumb; *i* = index finger; *m* = middle finger; *a* = third finger.

Fret-hand fingering is shown with the numbers **1 2 3 4**, normally to the left of the notehead.
0 indicates an open string.

String numbers are shown in a circle, normally below the note. For example, ⑥ = 6th string.

Finger-shifts are indicated by a small horizontal dash before the left-hand finger number.
For example, **2** followed by **-2** indicates that the 2nd finger can stay on the same string but move to another fret as a *guide finger*. The finger-shift sign should not be confused with a *slide* or *glissando* (where a longer dash joins two noteheads).

Slurs are indicated by a curved line between two notes of differing pitch. These should not be confused with *ties* (where two notes of the same pitch are joined by a curved line in order to increase the duration of the first note).

Half barrés (covering 2 to 4 strings) are shown like this: ½B, followed by a Roman numeral to indicate the fret position of the half barré. For example, ½BI indicates a half barré at the first fret. A dotted line will indicate the duration for which the barré should be held.

TECHNICAL WORK

The examiner will select some of the scales, arpeggios and chords shown below and ask the candidate to play them from memory. Scales and arpeggios should be played ascending and descending, i.e. from the lowest note to the highest and back again, without a pause and without repeating the top note. Chords should be played ascending only, and sounded string by string, starting with the lowest (root) note. To achieve a legato (i.e. smooth and over-ringing) sound, the whole chord shape should be fretted and kept on during playing. Chords and arpeggios should be played tirando, i.e. using free strokes.

To allow for flexibility in teaching approaches, the fingering suggestions given below are not compulsory and alternative systematic fingerings, that are musically effective, will be accepted. Suggested tempos are for general guidance only; slightly slower or faster performances will be acceptable, providing that the tempo is evenly maintained.

Overall, the examiner will be listening for accurate, even and clear playing. A maximum of **15** marks may be awarded in this section of the examination.

Recommended right hand fingering and tempo		
Scales:	alternating i m *or* m i;	apoyando (rest stroke) tempo ♩ = 144
1 octave arpeggios:	p i m a m i p;	tirando (free stroke) tempo ♩ = 116
2 octave arpeggios:	p i m a i m a (reverse descending); tirando	
Chords:	p on bass strings;	tirando tempo ♩ = 208
	i m a on the treble strings;	

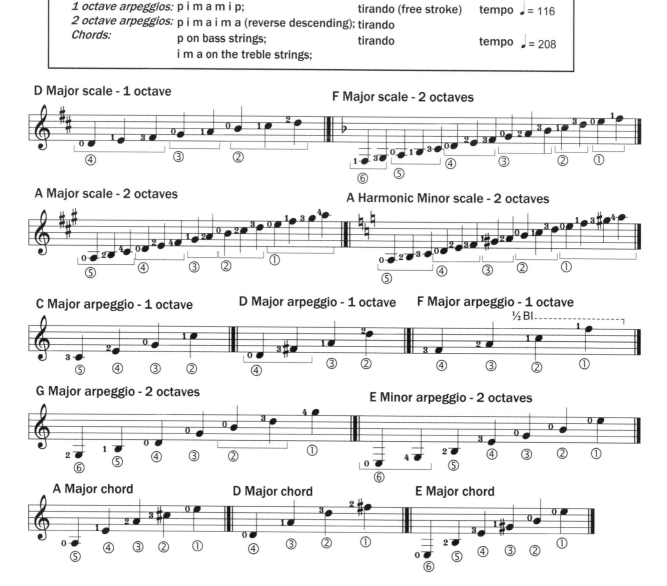

D Major scale - 1 octave

F Major scale - 2 octaves

A Major scale - 2 octaves

A Harmonic Minor scale - 2 octaves

C Major arpeggio - 1 octave

D Major arpeggio - 1 octave

F Major arpeggio - 1 octave

G Major arpeggio - 2 octaves

E Minor arpeggio - 2 octaves

A Major chord

D Major chord

E Major chord

PERFORMANCE

Candidates should play *one* melody from Group A and *two* contrasting pieces from Group B. A maximum of 60 marks may be awarded in this section of the examination – i.e. up to 20 marks for each performance. Fingering and tempo markings are for general guidance only and do not need to be adhered to strictly. All repeat markings should be followed.

Performance Tips

Melodies:

- Although some accidentals appear, all the melodies are in keys that relate to the range of scales that are required for this or lower grades and so practice of these scales would provide helpful preparation before attempting to play the melodies.

- Ensure that you identify, and bring out, the phrasing within each melody. The examiner will be listening for the demonstration of structured melodic shaping within each performance.

- In *See the Conquering Hero Comes* watch out for the B natural accidentals in bars 14 and 15. The D.C. al Fine marking indicates that once you've reached the end you should start again from the beginning and play until the end of bar 8 (where the marking Fine occurs).

- *Allegretto* has been arranged here in the key of D major and all the notes can be played from D major scale fingered in 'second position' (i.e. with the fret-hand position starting from the first finger at the second fret).

- The Elgar theme is best known as providing the musical basis for the song *Land Of Hope And Glory*. There are a few melodic differences between the two arrangements, such as the long notes in bars 1 and 5. This arrangement includes *first and second time endings*: the bars bracketed as ⌐1. (bars 13 - 16) should be omitted on the repeat playing and replaced with those bracketed as ⌐2. (bars 17 - 28). Watch out for the syncopated rhythm that occurs in bar 10 and is repeated in several other bars.

- *O Sole Mio* is a well-known Italian song written at the end of the 19th century. Some rubato can be used to capture the lyrical nature of the piece. The *tenuto marks* above the notes in bar 17 indicate that these notes should be held for their full value (or even lengthened a little) and emphasised slightly.

Canario *(Calvi):*

- This piece was originally written for baroque guitar. It is arranged in second position (with the first finger on the second fret), which suits the fingering required by the key of D major.

- A half barré is suggested in the second section, so that the A and C# notes can be played together without the need for a change of position.

Waltz *(Carulli):*

- Make sure that all the bass notes are held for their full value (normally dotted minims) and not cut short.

- In the first two sections (up to bar 16) the melody notes on the 3rd and 5th quaver beats (marked with tenuto marks) should be held and slightly emphasised. The repeated open G string throughout these sections is there just to give a sense of movement and it should not be played too loudly.

Andante *(Sor):*

- The piece begins with a C major chord for the first two bars. It would be helpful to position the full chord shape before commencing, and maintain the shape through these bars. The same principle can be applied in other places within the piece, such as in bars 8, 25-26 and 32.

- The repeated open G string that occurs in the middle voice of bars 9 to 23 is there just to give a sense of movement and harmonic contrast: it should not be played too loudly.

Allegro *(Giuliani):*

- The melody lies in the bass and should be brought out clearly. Most bars of this piece involve picking from a simple chord shape, followed by a short phrase in the bass (the notes of which alternate with a higher pedal note).

- The right-hand fingering that is given for the first bar can be maintained until bar 9 – from which point a simple pima fingering can be used.

Cameltrain *(Nuttall):*

- This piece features a *syncopated rhythm* throughout: in most bars a single bass note occurs on beat 1 with the first melody note coming after beat 1 and the second melody note coming after beat 2 – both on the 'off-beat'. This gives the piece a distinctive rhythmic character.

- Pairs of notes are often used in the melody – sometimes moving down a semitone (half step) and then up again, so you can often use the same fingers just moved down and up a fret.

Battle Drone *(Houghton):*

- This piece uses a D major key signature, but the repeated appearance of C natural accidentals indicates that the melody is based on the D Mixolydian modal scale – which, together with the $\frac{6}{8}$ time signature, gives it a slight Celtic character. If all the C notes are fretted on the G string then the entire piece can be played in second position.

- The opening bar (and other bars) features an open G *grace note*; this should be followed swiftly by a *hammer-on* (i.e. ascending slur) onto the main A note. Notice that this occurs again in bar 2 but with the dynamic marked as 'p' (softly); the composer states that this is "to symbolise the battle cries of the enemy in the distance".

Clown On A Horse *(Kiselev):*

- This light-hearted piece is in the key of A major, but features quite a lot of accidentals; in particular the alternation between C sharp and C natural helps to create a playful feel in the music.

- At the very end there is a startling percussive effect achieved by laying the fingers of the left hand across the strings to deaden them whilst the right hand fingers slap all the strings and the performer shouts out "oh".

Waltzing Matilda *(Trad.):*

- This is an arrangement by guitarist John Couch of this well-known Australian song, originally written around the very end of the 19th century.

- Ensure that the melody is clearly brought out and don't be afraid to use some *rubato* to help capture the lyrical character of the piece. The word *'rit'* that occurs in several places is an abbreviation of *'ritenuto'* which means "held back", i.e. change to a slower tempo for the duration marked.

See The Conquering Hero Comes

[Group A]

George Frideric Handel
(1685 – 1759)

Allegretto, from Symphony No. 6

[Group A]

Ludwig Van Beethoven
(1770 – 1827)

Pomp and Circumstance March No.1

[Group A]

Edward Elgar
(1857 – 1934)

O Sole Mio

[Group A]

Eduardo Di Capua
(1865 – 1917)

8

Canario

[Group B]

Carlo Calvi
(1612 – 1669)

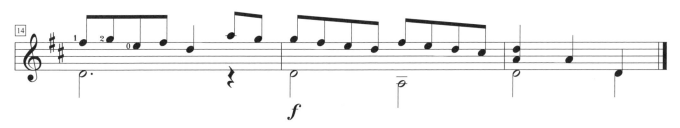

Waltz Op.121 No.1

[Group B]

Ferdinando Carulli
(1770 – 1841)

Andante Op.35 No.1

[Group B]

**Fernando Sor
(1778 - 1839)**

Allegro Op.50 No.13

[Group B]

Mauro Giuliani
(1781 - 1829)

12

Cameltrain

[Group B]

Peter Nuttall
(1949 –)

Battle Drone

Mark Houghton
(1959 –)

[Group B]

14

Clown On A Horse

[Group B]

Oleg Kiselev
(1964 –)

Left hand deadens the strings while
right hand fingers slap the strings

"Oh!"

Performer shout out

15

Waltzing Matilda

[Group B]

**Traditional
(c1900)**

16

VIVA VOCE

I n this section of the examination candidates will be engaged in a short discussion to enable the examiner to assess the candidate's understanding of musical rudiments and their responses to the pieces played. A maximum of 7 marks may be awarded.

At Grade Two candidates should be able to:

• name, and explain the meaning of, all basic notational elements in the music performed in the Performance component of the exam including stave, bars and bar-lines, clef, pitches of individual notes, rhythmic values of notes and rests (including dotted notes), key and time signatures, and (only if they occur in the performed music) accidentals, dynamics, articulation markings and any additional markings.

• explain which is their favourite piece and why.

• assign simple descriptive words to describe the mood of the pieces (e.g. happy, sad, gentle, lively).

Below are some examples of the *type* of questions that the examiner may ask at Grade Two. Note that these are examples only; the list is by no means exhaustive and candidates should not simply learn these answers by rote. The wording and phrasing of the questions may vary even when the same topic is involved.

Question: What is this extra line below the stave called?

Answer: A leger line.

Question: What is the pitch of this note? (Examiner points to a note on the first leger line above the stave.)

Answer: A.

Question: What is the time signature of this piece?

Answer: ¾ time, three crotchet beats per bar.

Question: What type of note is this, and how many beats does it last for? (Examiner points to a dotted minim.)

Answer: It is a dotted minim (or dotted half note) and it lasts for three crotchet (or quarter) beats.

Question: What does the dot after the note mean?

Answer: It increases its length by half as much again.

Question: What does this sign mean? (Examiner points to a decrescendo mark.)

Answer: It means 'get quieter'.

Question: What is this and what does it mean? (Examiner points to the key signature.)

Answer: It is the key signature for D major and it indicates that all the F notes should be played as F# and all the C notes should be played as C#.

Question: What does Andante mean?

Answer: At a 'walking pace'.

Question: Which of the three pieces that you played today is your favourite and why?

Answer: *Waltzing Matilda*, because I can play it with a lot of feeling and also it's a piece everyone recognises when I play it.

Question: How would you describe the overall mood of Canario?

Answer: It's bright and lively.

Some useful information relating to this section of the examination is provided below.

Major and Minor Key signatures

| F Major or D Minor | C Major or A Minor | G Major or E Minor | D Major or B Minor | A Major or F♯ Minor |

Time signatures
The time signatures that occur at this grade are:

$\frac{2}{4}$ = 2 crotchet beats per bar. Also known as *simple duple time.*

$\frac{3}{4}$ = 3 crotchet beats per bar. *Simple triple time.*

$\frac{4}{4}$ = 4 crotchet beats per bar. This can also be indicated by $\mathbf{C}$. *Simple quadruple time.*

$\frac{2}{2}$ = 2 minim beats per bar. This can also be indicated by $\mathbf{\mathcal{C}}$. *Simple duple time.*

$\frac{6}{8}$ = 6 quavers per bar, but with a pulse of 2 dotted crotchets per bar. Also known as *compound duple time.*

Common Terms and signs
Candidates should have an understanding of any terms and signs that appear in the music performed. Some examples are given below.

D. C. al Fine   repeat from the beginning up to the point marked *Fine* (the end).

D. C. al Coda   repeat from the beginning up to the sign ⊕ , then go straight to the Coda (end section).

♩ = 100   metronome tempo (e.g. 100 crotchet beats per minute).

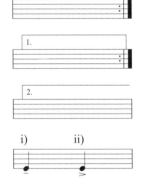

Repeat sign. (Play from the previous 2 vertical dots, or, in their absence, from the beginning.)

First time ending. (On the first playing, play the notes below this box.)

Second time ending. (On the second playing, omit the first time ending and play from this bar.)

i) *Tenuto sign* – to be held for its full value and slightly emphasised.
ii) *Accent* – this (marcato) accent sign indicates that the note should be stressed by playing strongly.

Tempo terms

Rall. (*rallentando*)	becoming gradually slower
Rit. (*ritenuto*)	held back
Andante	at a 'walking' pace
Allegro	at a fast and lively pace
Allegretto	rather lively (less so than Allegro)

Dynamics

pp	*p*	*mp*	*mf*	*f*	*ff*
pianissimo	*piano*	*mezzo-piano*	*mezzo-forte*	*forte*	*fortissimo*
very soft	soft	medium soft	medium loud	loud	very loud

crescendo (cresc.) – getting louder

decrescendo (decresc.) / diminuendo – getting softer

SIGHT READING

The examiner will show you the sight reading test and allow you up to one minute preparation time before performing it. A maximum of 10 marks may be awarded in this section of the examination. The table below shows the range of the piece:

Length	Keys	Time signatures	Note values	Fingerboard positions
4 bars	Major: C, G, D Minor: A, E, B	2 3 4 4 4 4	o 𝅗𝅥 𝅗𝅥 𝅘𝅥. 𝅘𝅥 𝅘𝅥𝅮	1st / 2nd

Sight Reading Tips

1. Always check the key and time signature BEFORE you start to play.

2. Once you have identified the key it is helpful to remember that the notes will all come from the key scale – which you should already know from the Technical Work section of this handbook. This means that it will generally be easier to play the sight reading if you use the same fingering as you have used for playing the scale.

3. Before you start to play, quickly scan through the piece and check any notes or rhythms that you are unsure of.

4. Note the tempo or style marking, but be careful to play at a tempo at which you can maintain accuracy throughout.

5. Once you start to play, try and keep your eyes on the music. Avoid the temptation to keep looking at the fingerboard – that's a sure way to lose your place in the music.

6. If you do make an error, try not to let it affect your confidence for the rest of the piece. It is better to keep going and capture the overall shape of the piece, rather than stopping and going back to correct errors.

The following examples show the *type* of pieces that will be presented in the examination.

(i) Moderato

(ii) Allegro

(iii) Adagio

(iv) Moderato

(v) Andante

(vi) Adagio

(vii) Moderato

(viii) Lento

AURAL TESTS

A maximum of 8 marks may be awarded in this section of the examination. The tests will be played by the examiner on either guitar or piano, at the examiner's discretion. The examples below are shown in guitar notation and give a broad indication of the type of tests that will be given during the examination. Candidates wishing to view sample tests in piano notation should obtain the current LCM Exams *Specimen Aural Tests* booklet.

Rhythm tests

1a. After the examiner has played a short harmonised piece of music, similar to one of the examples below, the candidate will be asked to identify the time signature as *3* or *4* time.

1b. The examiner will play the piece again. The candidate should beat in time (i.e. conduct – not just clap or tap) with the examiner's playing.

> **How to beat time.**
> Begin with your arm out in front of you, with your hand at eye level. The first beat of each bar should be shown by a strong downwards motion of the arm. In 3 time, move the arm to the right for beat two and return to the top of your 'triangle' for beat three. 4 time will involve a horizontal move to the left for beat two and to the right for beat three; the final fourth beat being a return upwards to your starting position. If you are left-handed, you should swap the left and right motions.

1c. The examiner will play one bar of the piece again in a single line version. The candidate will be asked to identify the note values, such as in the example below (which is taken from bar 3 of the first example above).

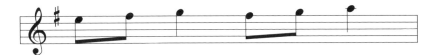

2 quavers (eighth notes), 1 crotchet (quarter note), 2 quavers (eighth notes), 1 crotchet (quarter note). Contemporary or traditional terminology can be used to describe the note values.

Pitch tests

2a. The examiner will play a major or minor triad followed by one of the notes of the chord alone. The candidate should identify the note as either "bottom, middle or top", or by sol-fa (Doh, Mi, Soh) or interval number (root, 3rd, 5th) if preferred.

2b. The chord will be played again and the candidate will be asked if the chord was major or minor.

major   (middle, mi, 3rd)   minor   (top, soh, 5th)   minor   (bottom, doh, 1st)

2c. The candidate will be asked to identify, either by letter name or sol-fa or interval number, any of the first five notes of the C, G, D or F major scales. The key will be named and the tonic chord played, followed by the the first five notes of the scale in ascending order. The examiner will then play any ONE of these notes again for the candidate to identify.

A / Re / 2nd   F♯ / Mi / 3rd

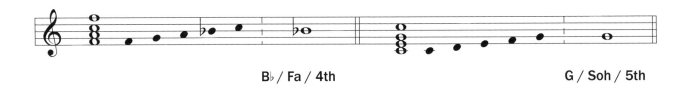

B♭ / Fa / 4th   G / Soh / 5th

LCM
LONDON COLLEGE OF MUSIC

Classical Guitar
Examination Entry Form

GRADE TWO
or Leisure Play Elementary

The standard LCM Exams music entry form is NOT valid for Classical Guitar entries.
Entry to the examination is only possible via this original form.
Photocopies of this form will not be accepted under any circumstances.

Please use black ink and block capital letters when completing this form.

Circle the type of examination you wish to enter: • Grade examination   • Leisure Play examination.

SESSION (Spring/Summer/Winter): _____ YEAR: _____

Preferred Examination Centre (if known): _____
If left blank you will be examined at the nearest venue to your home address.

Candidate Details:

Candidate Name (as to appear on certificate):

_____

Candidate ID (if entered previously): _____ Date of birth: _____

Gender (M/F): _____ Ethnicity (see chart overleaf): _____

Date of birth and ethnicity details are for statistical purposes only, and are not passed on to the examiner.

☐ Tick this box if you are attaching details of particular needs requirements.

Teacher Details:

Teacher Name (as to appear on certificate): _____

Teacher Qualifications (if required on certificate): _____

LCM Teacher Code (if entered previously): _____

Address: _____

_____ Postcode: _____

Tel. No. (day): _____ (evening): _____

☐ Tick this box if any details above have changed since your last LCM entry.

IMPORTANT NOTES

- It is the candidate's responsibility to have knowledge of, and comply with, the current syllabus requirements. Where candidates are entered for examinations by a teacher, the teacher must take responsibility that candidates are entered in accordance with the current syllabus requirements. Failure to carry out any of the examination requirements may lead to disqualification.

- For candidates with particular needs, a letter giving details and requests for any special requirements (e.g. enlarged sight reading), together with an official supporting document (e.g. medical certificate), should be attached.

- Examinations may be held on any day of the week, including weekends. Any appointment requests (e.g. 'prefer morning,' or 'prefer weekdays') must be made at the time of entry. **LCM Exams and its Representatives will take note of the information given; however, no guarantees can be made that all wishes can be met.**

- Submission of this entry is an undertaking to abide by the current regulations.

ETHNIC ORIGIN CLASSIFICATIONS	
White	
01	British
02	Irish
03	Other white background
Mixed	
04	White and black Caribbean
05	White and black African
06	White and Asian
07	Other mixed background
Asian or Asian British	
08	Indian
09	Pakistani
10	Bangladeshi
11	Other Asian background
Black or Black British	
12	Caribbean
13	African
14	Other black background
Chinese or Other Ethnic Group	
15	Chinese
16	Other
17	**Prefer not to say**

Examination Fee: £ _____

Late Entry Fee (if necessary) £ _____

Total amount submitted: £ _____

Cheques or postal orders should be made payable to '*Thames Valley University*'.

A list of current fees, entry deadlines and session dates is available from LCM Exams.

Where to submit your entry form

Entries for public centres should be sent to the
**LCM Exams local examination centre representative
(NOT to the LCM Exams Head Office).**

View the LCM Exams website www.tvu.ac.uk/lcmexams
or contact the LCM Exams office (tel: 020 8231 2364 / email: lcm.exams@tvu.ac.uk)
for details of your nearest local examination centre representative.

Entries for the London area only, or for private centres, should be sent direct to:
LCM Exams, Thames Valley University, Walpole House, 18-22 Bond St, London, W5 5AA

Official Entry Form